Where Does It Go?

FARTS, FUMES AND OTHER GASES

Written by Helen Greathead
Illustrated by Kyle Beckett

Gareth Stevens
PUBLISHING

Please visit our website, www.garethstevens.com. For a free color catalog of all our high-quality books, call toll free 1-800-542-2595 or fax 1-877-542-2596.

Cataloging-in-Publication Data

Names: Greathead, Helen, author. | Beckett, Kyle, illustrator.
Title: Farts, fumes, and other gases / Helen Greathead, illustrated by Kyle Beckett.
Description: Buffalo, NY : Gareth Stevens Publishing, 2026. | Series: Where does it go? | Includes glossary and index.
Identifiers: ISBN 9781482475784 (pbk.) | ISBN 9781482475791 (library bound) | ISBN 9781482475807 (ebook)
Subjects: LCSH: Gases--Juvenile literature.
Classification: LCC QC161.2 G724 2026 | DDC 533--dc2

Published in 2026 by
Gareth Stevens Publishing
2544 Clinton St.
Buffalo, NY 14224

First published in Great Britain in 2023 by Wayland

Commissioning Editor: Elise Short
Editor: Nicola Edwards
Designer: Anthony Hannant, Little Red Ant
Science consultant: Peter Riley

Printed in China
CPSIA compliance information: Batch #QW26GS: For further information contact Gareth Stevens at 1-800-542-2595.

Find us on

CONTENTS

WHAT ON EARTH ARE GASES?

Gases are around you all the time. They are hard to spot because they often have no color or smell – although there's a gas in some farts that definitely does smell. But what are gases and where do they go? Let's investigate!

Most things on Earth are made up of particles that are too small to see. Particles in something that is solid have a regular pattern. Solids are things like:

The particles in something that is liquid can move around and flow over each other. Liquids can be poured. Liquids are things like:

The particles in gases move all over the place, they spread out and keep on moving. When they crash into something they set off in another direction.

The air you breathe is mostly made up of nitrogen and oxygen gases.

Farts happen when some gases inside your body need to get out ...

WHAT GOES IN ...

Pee-u! Was that you? Don't be embarrassed. Everybody farts. Farts are caused by a build up of gases in your body.

How farts start

When you eat food, you take in great gulps of air.

Bacteria in your intestines help break the food down into parts your body can and can't use.

Some of the useless parts are gases. These gases mix with gases from the air you swallowed.

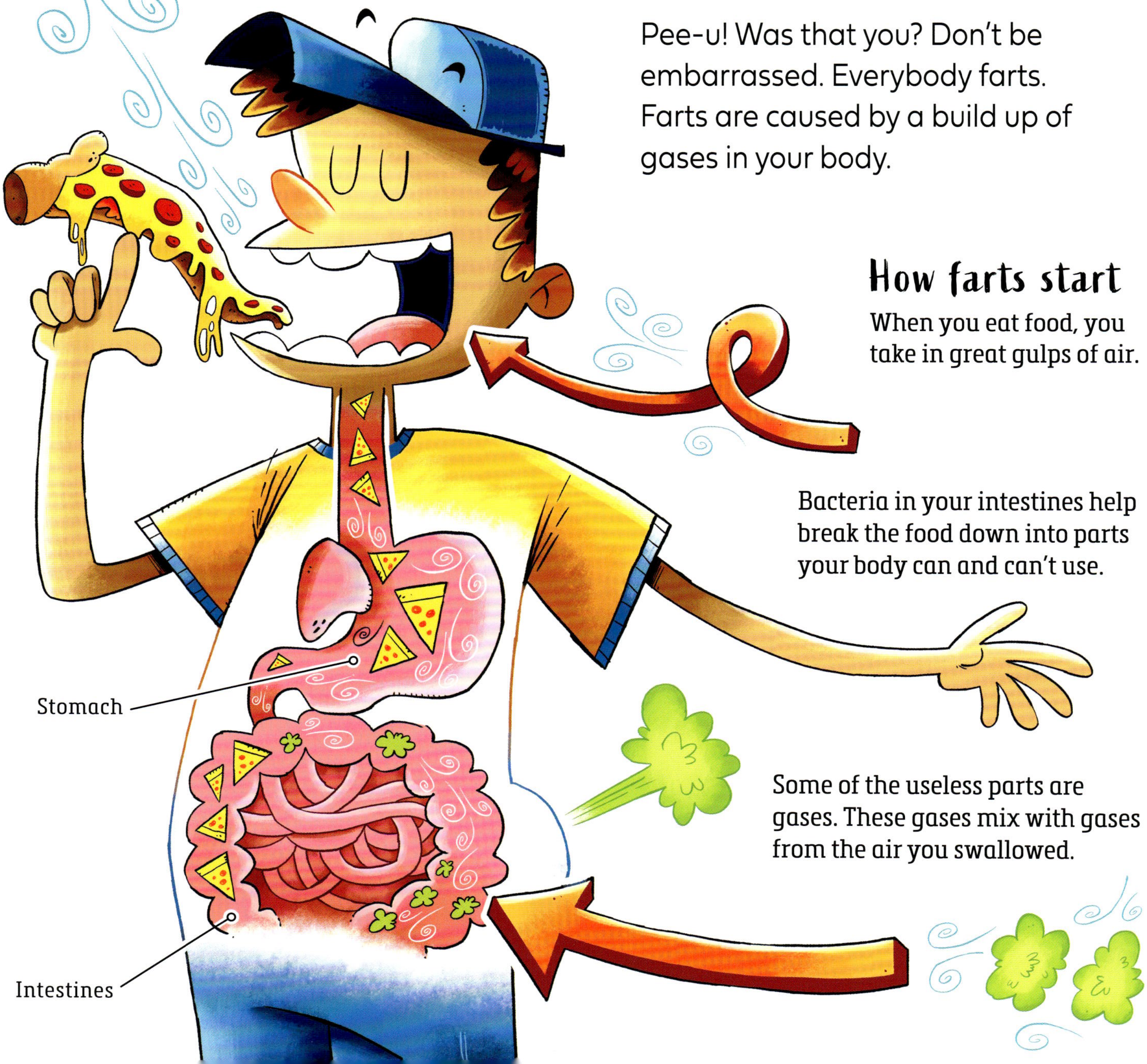

Your body gets rid of gases it doesn't need by pushing them out through your bottom – at **6.8 miles (11 km) per hour**. That's faster than you can walk!

How many farts a day?

Australian scientists discovered that:

- Women fart between **one** and **32 times** a day
- Men fart between **two** and **53 times** a day
- Men's farts are smellier!

Gassy fact
The scientific name for farting is flatulence.

What's in a fart?

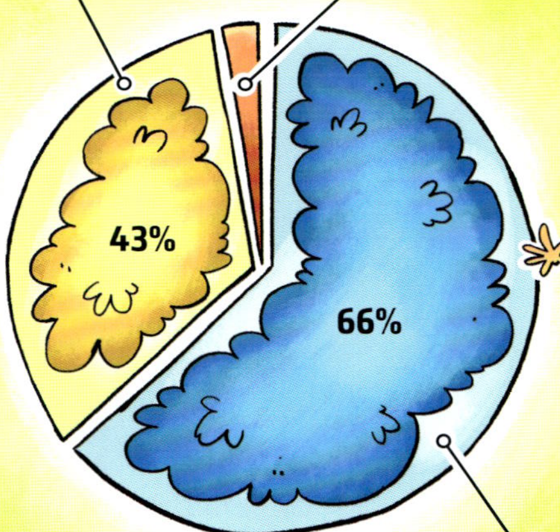

WHAT'S THAT SMELL?

When you're full of beans, you're full of healthy proteins, fiber ... and farts. The fiber in beans helps you poop regularly, but it's difficult to digest. So how do beans make you gassy?

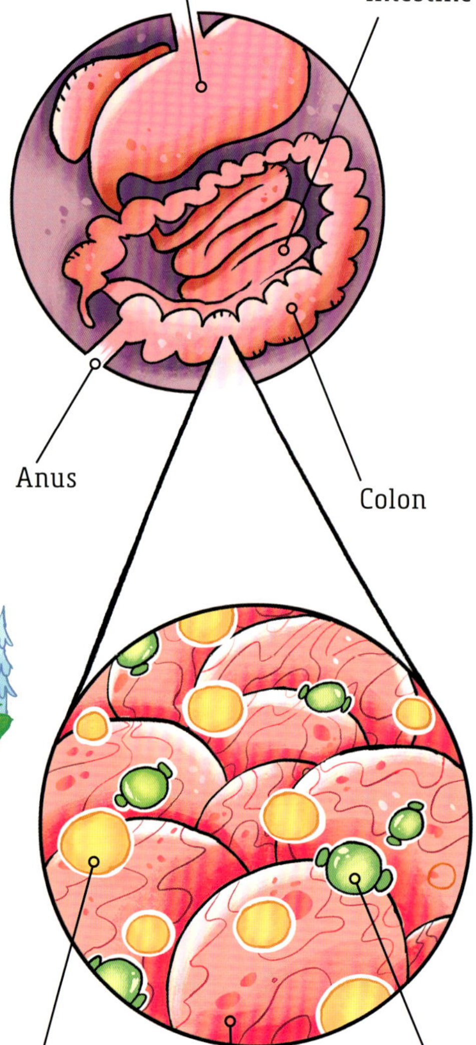

Bacteria in the colon feast on the bean fiber and produce hydrogen gas. Most beans contain sulfur (see page 26) that mixes with the hydrogen to make hydrogen sulfide – and farts that smell.

Foods that cause smelly farts:

Fizzy farts

Fizzy drinks like soda contain bubbles of CO_2 gas. Gassy bubbles build up in your gut and come out as a burp or a fart.

Gas comes out as a burp *before* and a fart *after* it reaches the colon.

You fart *more* if you:

- Drink fizzy pop through a straw
- Move around while you drink.

You fart *less* if you:

- Drink slowly
- Drink plenty of water.

WINDY WILDLIFE

It isn't just humans who are gassy. Animals and plants fart too. Some put their farts to good use ...

Insects let fly

Beaded lacewings lay their eggs in termite nests. When the larvae hatch out and get hungry, they fart out a gas that can paralyze six termites at a time. Then they eat the termites!

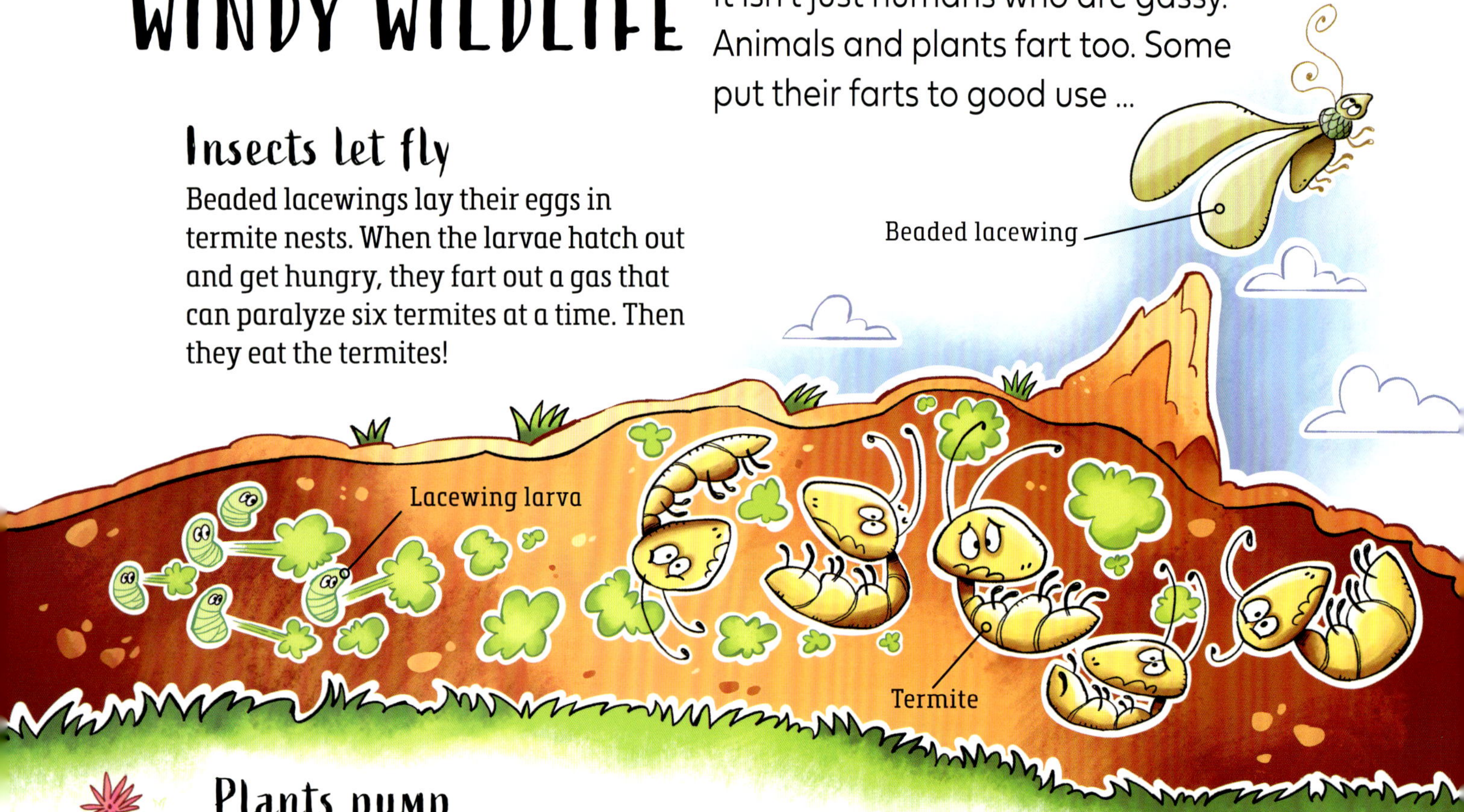

Plants pump

The roots of some mimosa plants are lined with little sacks. When a human or animal touches the root, these sacks fart out a bad-egg stink. Scientists think this plant fart is to put off predators.

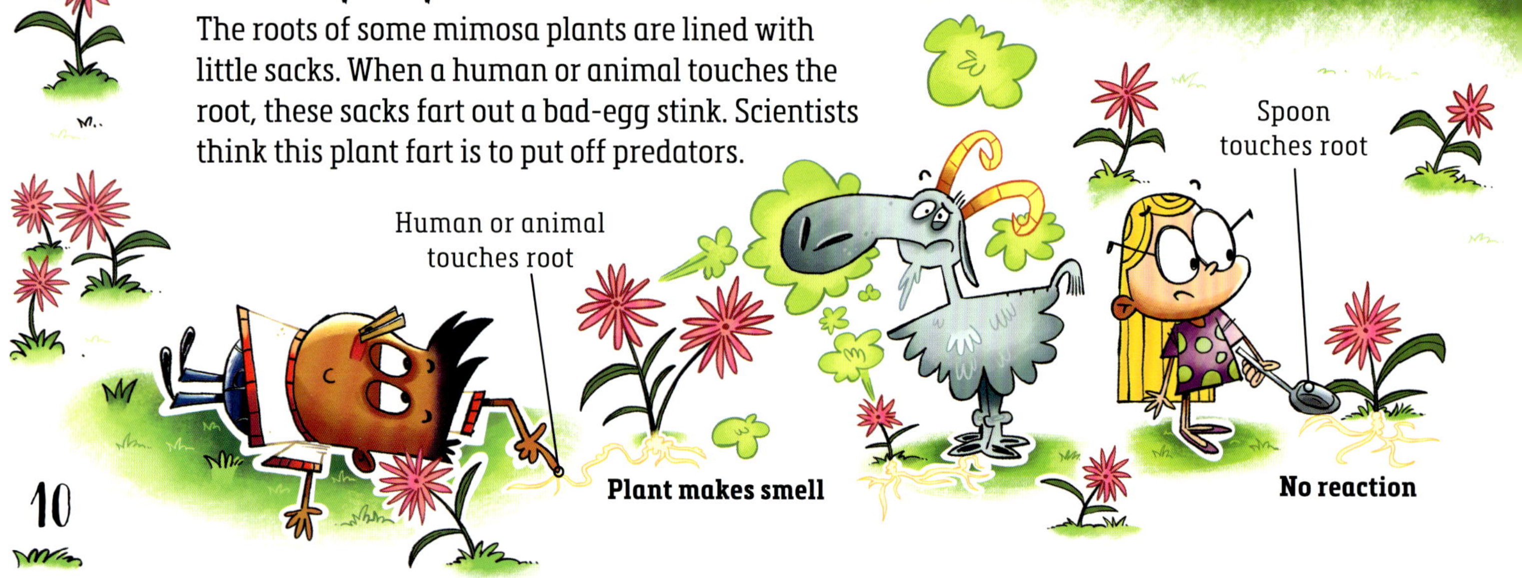

Fish fart

In the 1990s, the Swedish Navy heard strange hissing and popping sounds in the ocean and blamed enemy submarines. Scientists found that the noises were actually herring farts!

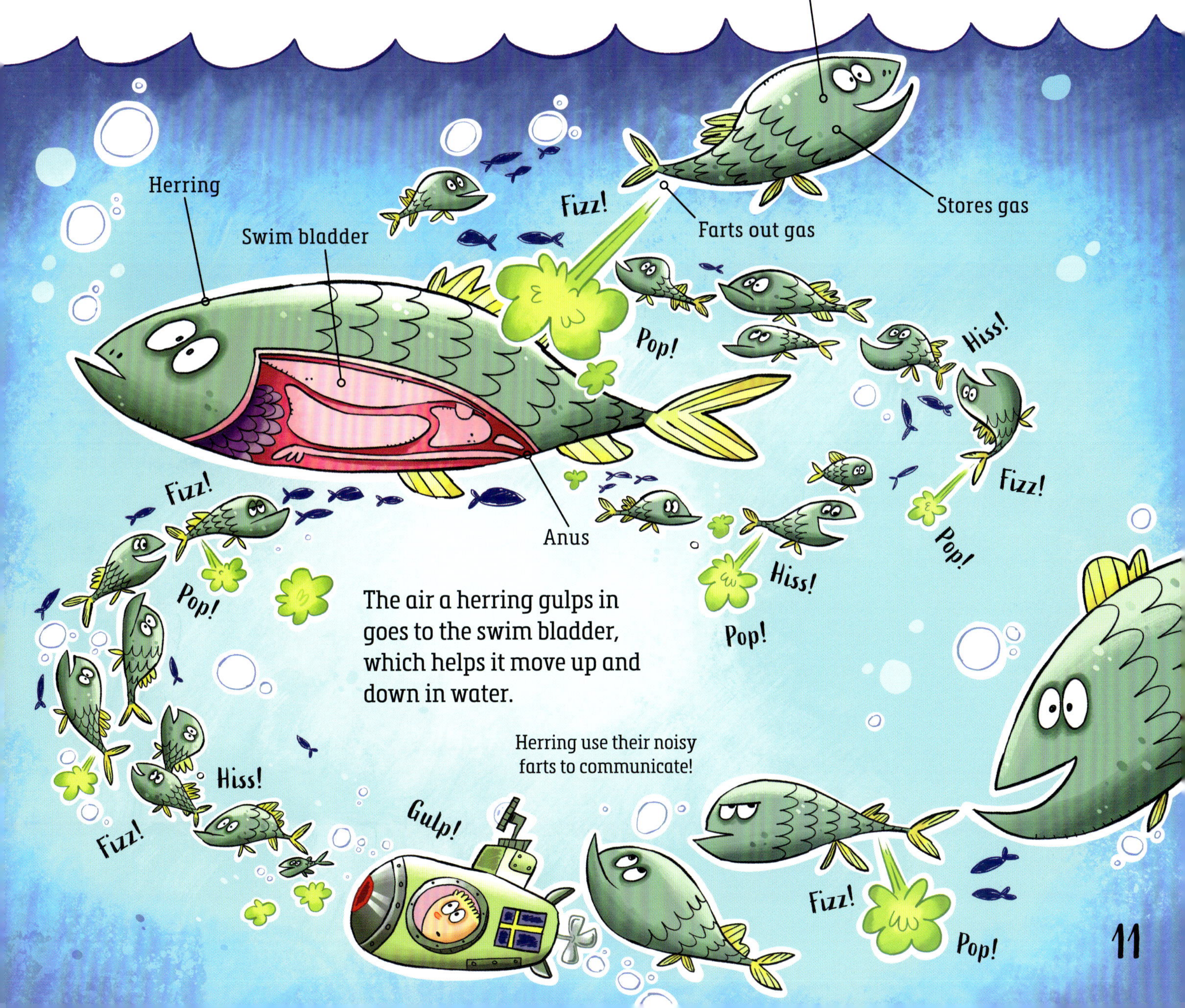

The air a herring gulps in goes to the swim bladder, which helps it move up and down in water.

Herring use their noisy farts to communicate!

WHAT ARE GREENHOUSE GASES?

Without greenhouse gases (GHGs), Earth would be a chilly -2.2°F (-19°C). Brr! GHGs in Earth's atmosphere trap warmth from the sun, keeping Earth at just the right temperature. But too many greenhouse gases cause changes in the normal weather. This is called climate change.

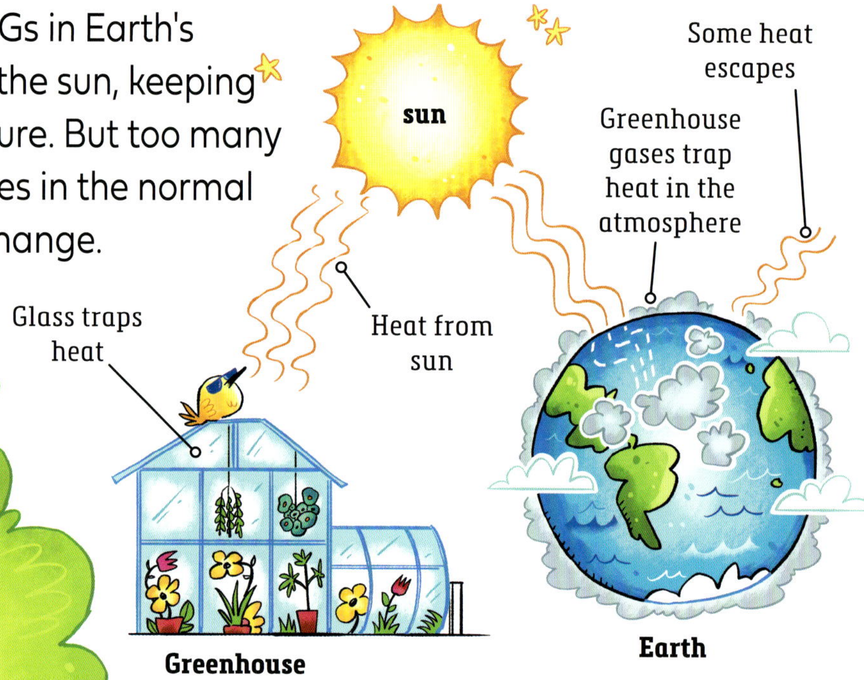

GHGs include:

- **Water vapor**
- **CO_2**
- **Methane**
- **Ozone** (see pages 16–17)
- **Factory-made CFCs** (chlorofluorocarbons, see pages 16–17)
- **Nitrous oxide**

Most GHGs are found naturally on Earth.

All living things breathe out CO_2.

Methane gas can come from rotting plants in wetlands. It's also burped up by cows (see pages 18-19).

Gassy fact

Human activity adds ***44 billion tons (40 billion mt)*** of CO_2 to the atmosphere each year.

And methane can hang around in the atmosphere for eight years before chemical reactions turn it into CO_2 and water. In that time methane traps LOTS of heat. It's ***28 times*** more powerful than CO_2.

But some CO_2 stays in the atmosphere, trapping heat for 100 to 1,000 years!

Because of our activities, humans create more CO_2 and methane than Earth needs. We're making the planet too warm. So how do we use gases?

GASSY HOMES

We use gases at home every day.
So where do they hide ...?

A kettle produces steam when water boils. Steam is a gas that scientists call **water vapor**.

Natural gas makes nearly half of North America's electricity. It can be dangerous, but you can't see or smell it. Some countries add a rotten-egg stink to it, so if there's a leak, people know!

Natural gas is mostly **methane**. Methane burns easily so it's great for cooking and heating.

Natural gas is a fossil fuel found deep underground. It comes from plants and animals that died millions of years ago. Pipelines carry it to your kitchen.

Argon gas is pumped in between the panes of glass in double-glazed windows. It's heavier than air, so heat travels through it more slowly, keeping warmth inside.

Helium gas inside the balloon is lighter than air. That's why it floats!

Nitrogen gas is pumped into food packaging, pushing out oxygen. Food doesn't react to nitrogen, meaning mold and bacteria are slow to grow.

There are gases in your fridge as well as food ...

WHAT'S IN YOUR FRIDGE?

Manufactured gases were once used to keep home fridges cool. These CFC gases didn't harm humans or catch fire easily. They seemed safe!

In the 1970s, scientists realized that CFCs were not safe after all ...

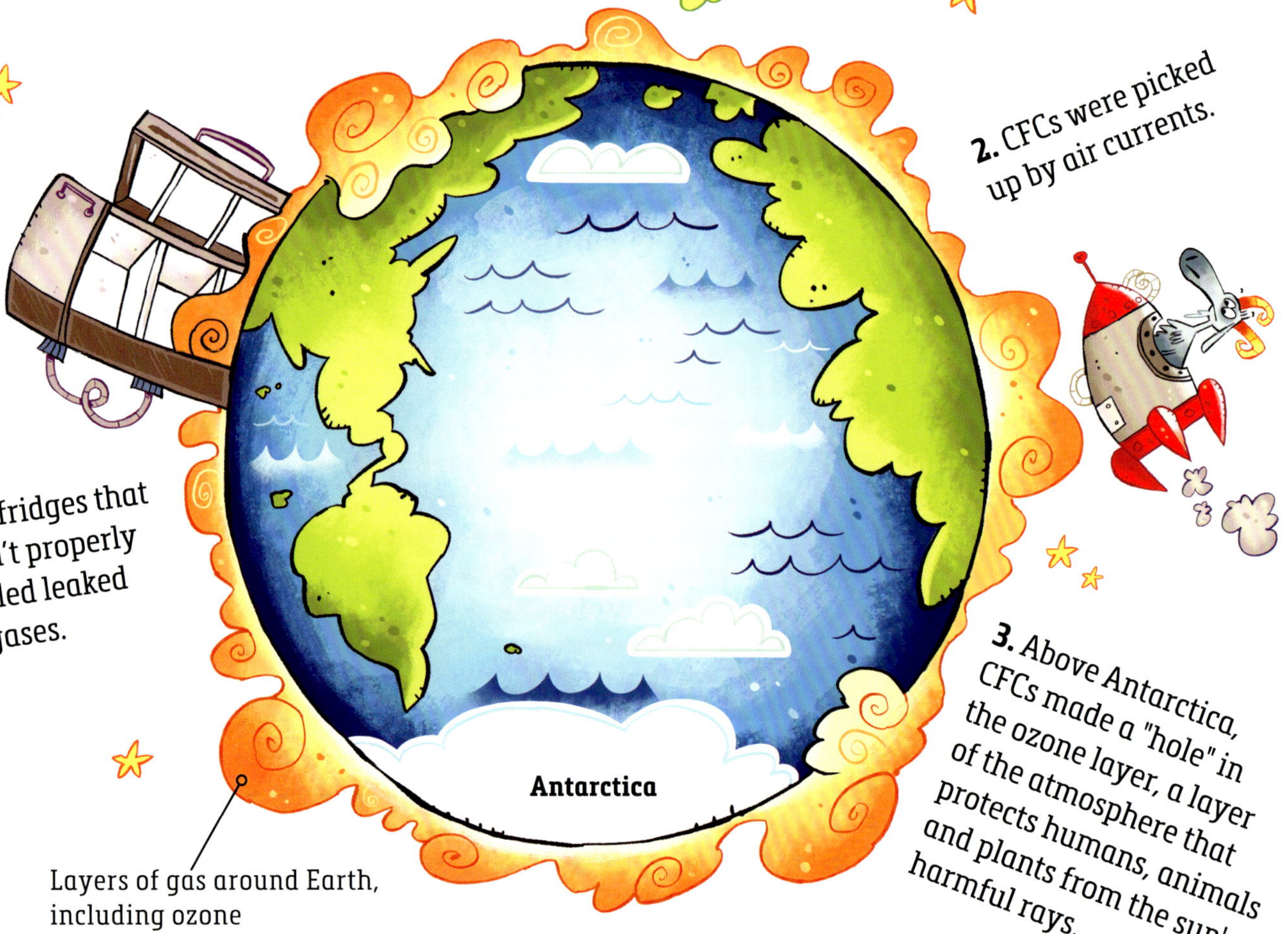

sun

2 years – The time CFCs take to reach the stratosphere

50–100 years – How long they stay there

Stratosphere containing ozone layer

Here's what happens when CFC molecules meet ozone molecules:

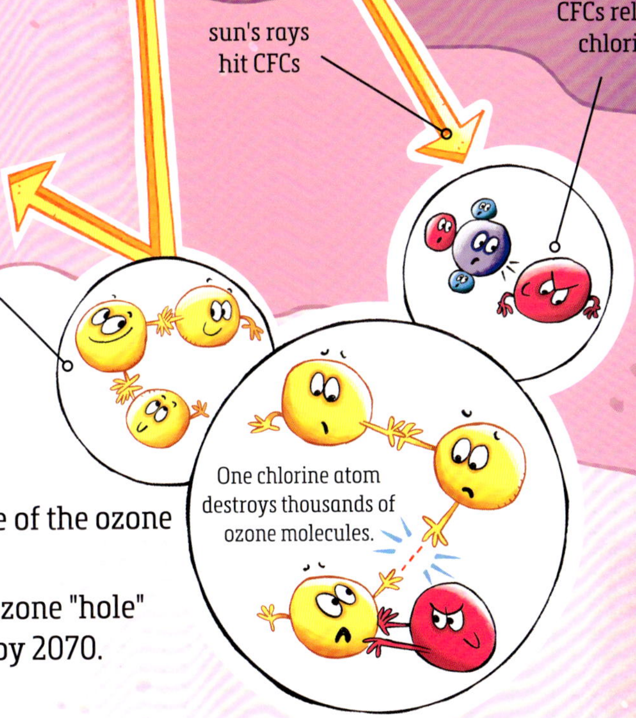

The world agreed to stop using CFCs in 1987.

10.2 million miles² (26.6 million km²): the size of the ozone "hole" in 2006.

3 million miles² (8 million km²): how big the ozone "hole" should be by 2040. It could recover completely by 2070.

Troposphere

Sadly there are plenty more gases causing problems for the planet ...

Earth

THE TROUBLE WITH COW BURPS

Now that we know about farts (see pages 4-11), what about gassy burps? Cows burp a lot! They get rid of much more gas through burps than through farts. They burp every 90 seconds!

Where burps begin

Because a cow has to digest tough foods, like grasses and grains, it needs FOUR compartments in its stomach. Burps begin in the first part of the stomach, called the rumen.

Microbes in the rumen break food down so the cow absorbs the parts it needs. The microbes give off gases the cow can't digest. Burping sets those gases free.

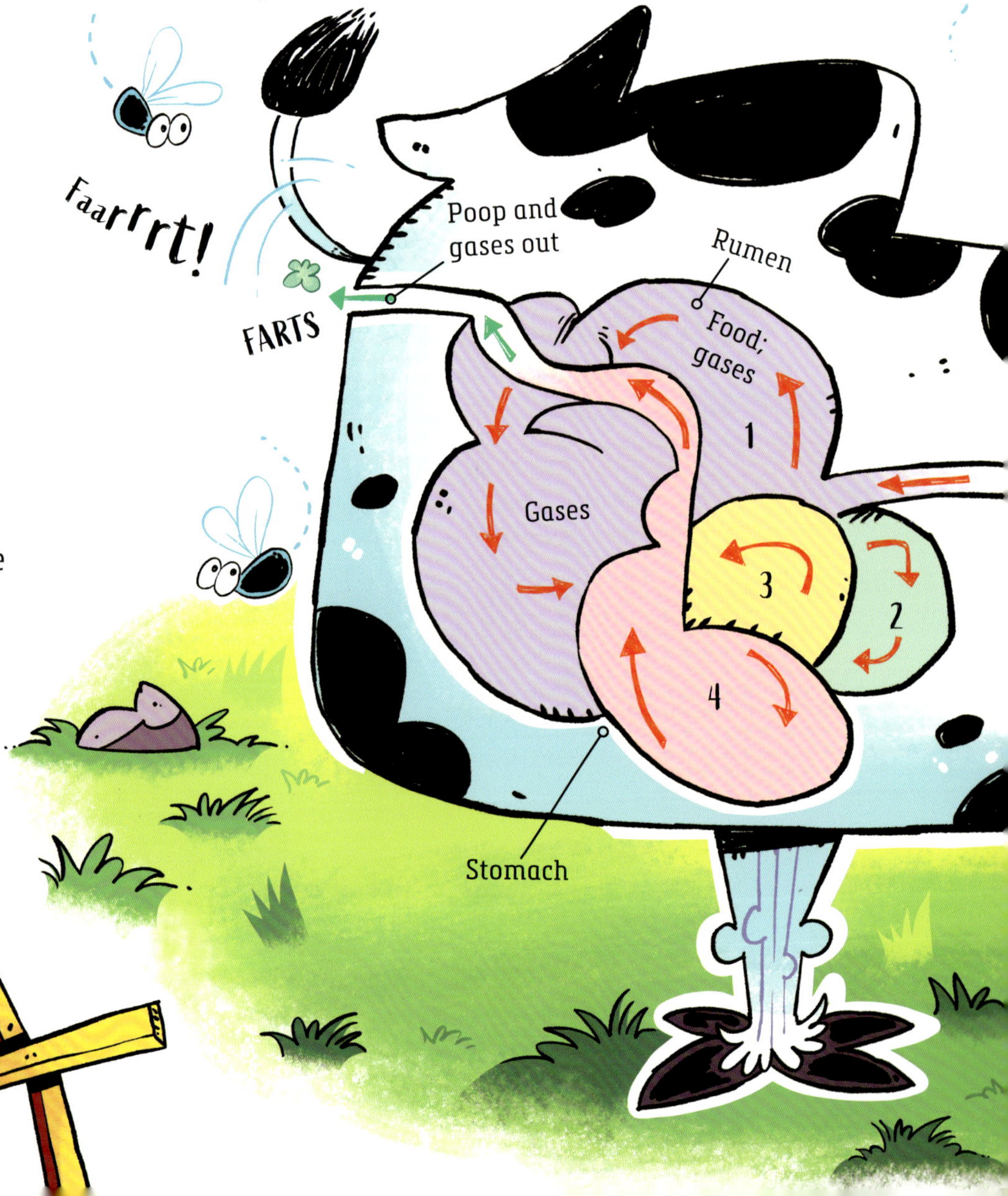

Gassy fact: The scientific name for a burp is an eructation.

Why burps are bad

Cows' burps contain the gases methane and CO_2 that we know can be harmful for the planet (see pages 12-13).

There are over **1.4 billion** cows on Earth. That's a lot of burps!

MESSING WITH METHANE

Scientists have interesting ideas for managing methane emissions.

The Burp-Catcher

This cow mask reduces emissions by ***53 percent!*** It catches the methane cows burp out and releases it as less harmful CO_2. The mask even connects to a mobile phone! Farmers get a personal profile of each cow...

Garlic and seaweed

Scientists tried adding red seaweed or extracts of garlic and citrus fruits to cattle feed – and reduced emissions by ***up to 70 percent.*** At first cows didn't like the taste of seaweed, and they produced less milk. They produced more milk with the garlic and citrus feed ... and were bothered by fewer flies!

Scientists had to be careful that the amount of garlic and citrus they added didn't change the milk's flavor.

Methane-zappers

Fifty percent of the world's population eats rice every day.

Bacteria in the paddy fields, where rice grows, belch out masses of methane. But German and Danish scientists hope that by injecting a different bacteria called cable bacteria into the soggy soil, they might cut methane emissions by ***over 90 percent!***

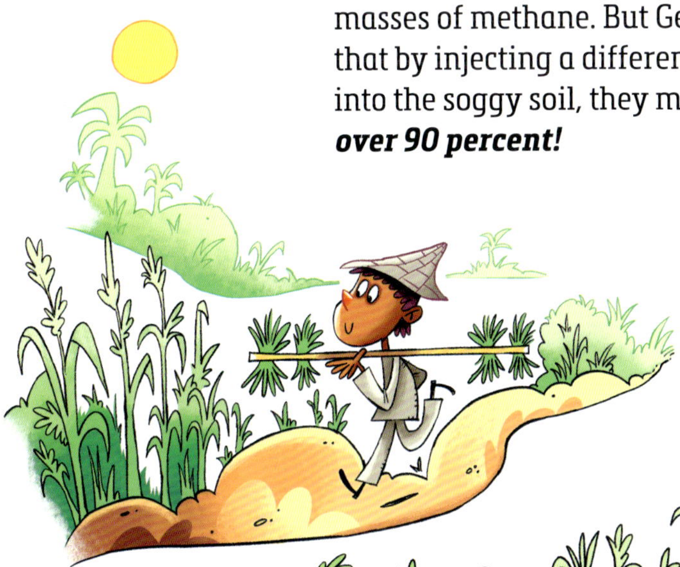

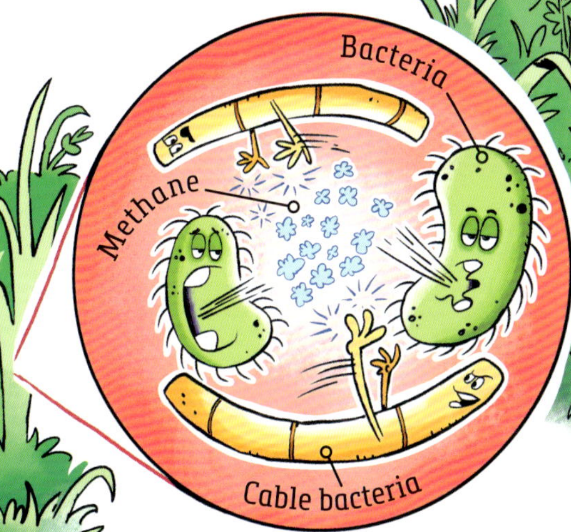

Cable bacteria make methane-producing bacteria harmless.

GASSY TRANSPORTATION

We need vehicles to get us to school, deliver our packages, and take us on vacation. But most of the vehicles we use today are a real polluting problem!

Ground control

Most road vehicles run by burning fossil fuels (gas or diesel). They belch out toxic gases that include:

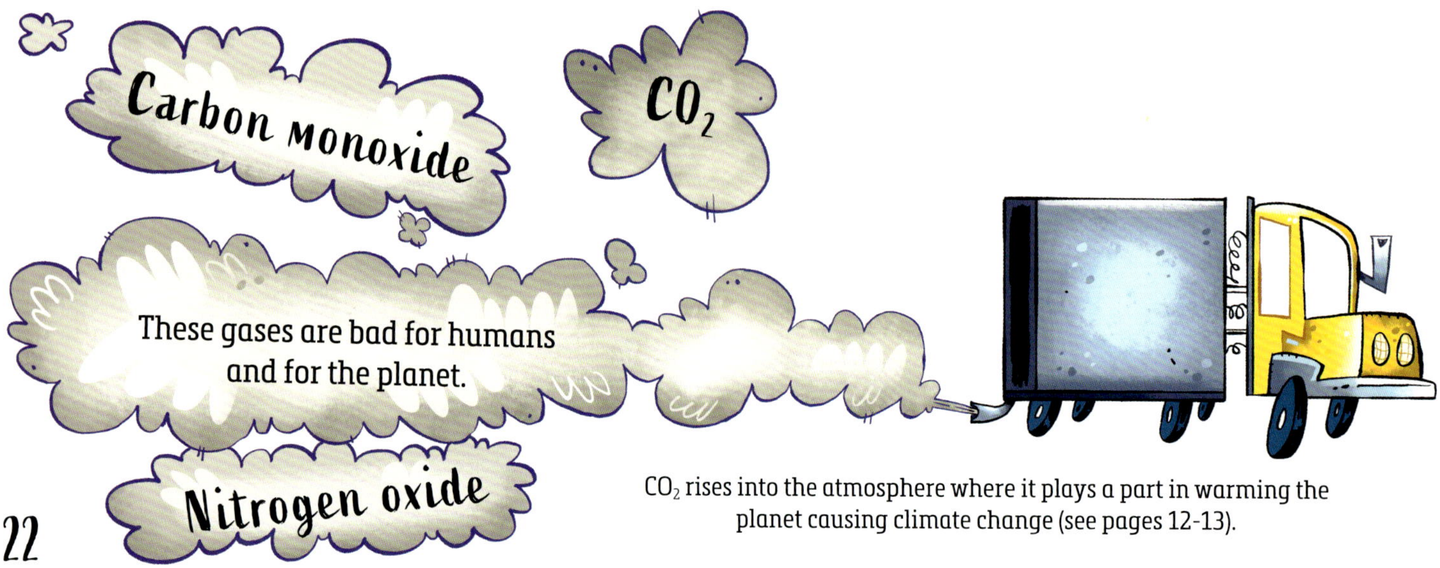

CO_2 rises into the atmosphere where it plays a part in warming the planet causing climate change (see pages 12-13).

Scary air

Airplanes fart out ***100 times*** more fumes each hour than buses or trains. Their vapor trails are made from water vapor that contains these gases:

CO_2 – Sulfur dioxide – Nitrogen oxide

The gases pollute the air. Their tiny particles fall to the ground and can be breathed in by humans.

Pollution from an airplane in Europe, flying above the clouds, can be whisked eastwards by the winds. It will reach India –6,210 miles (10,000 km) away!

When sunlight hits nitrogen oxide close to the ground, it creates a smoky fog or "smog." The smog carries dangerous particles that can make eyes burn and damage lungs.

Can we change how we travel?

FUEL SOLUTIONS

Most countries think plug-in electric vehicles (EVs), that don't belch out fumes, answer their greenhouse gas problem.

By **2030** all new cars sold in India will be electric.

An EV – as long as it is charged with renewable electricity – can be 90 percent cleaner than a fume-belching car.

In Sweden people often charge their cars at night, when the wind is strongest, to use renewable energy.

Flying bananas

Scientists converted powdered banana peel into hydrogen (and a solid type of carbon that can be used as fertilizer) using flashes of xenon gas. It took milliseconds!

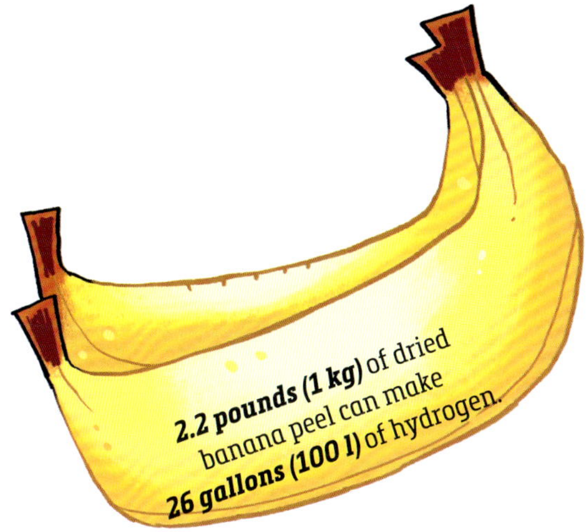

Burning hydrogen fuel produces water instead of CO_2, so this is "clean" energy, as long as the energy used to produce it is also clean.

Hydrogen gas has no smell. But hold your nose, because the next gas stinks!

BEAUTIFULLY SMELLY

Coal fires, car exhausts, and oil refineries belch out a gas that we also use to treat some foods. Sulfur dioxide, the gas that makes farts smell (see pages 8-9), helps raisins, sugar, and soft drinks last longer.

Smelly poisons

On Kawah Ijen volcano, on the Indonesian island of Java, men still risk their lives to mine solid sulfur by hand.

Cracks in the rock spit out stinky clouds of sulfur dioxide gas and deadly, poisonous hydrogen sulfide.

Miners carry lumps of yellow rock away. Sulfur dioxide will be extracted from it for white table sugar.

Burning blue

There's no oxygen under the rock. When the gas bursts out and hits oxygen in the air, some catches fire and burns with a bright blue flame. Some cools to a red liquid then to yellow rock.

At night, tourists watch the flames on this smelly, but beautiful, mountain!

Gases in the air can make other colors too ...

SKY-HIGH DISCO

Gases we use on the ground rise up into the atmosphere. Sometimes you can see them glowing green, red, pink, and blue. They stretch hundreds of miles across the night sky. They're called the Northern Lights at the North Pole and the Southern Lights at the South Pole.

Earth is protected by a magnetic field. When storms happen on the sun, they whip up huge clouds of particles that travel millions of miles.

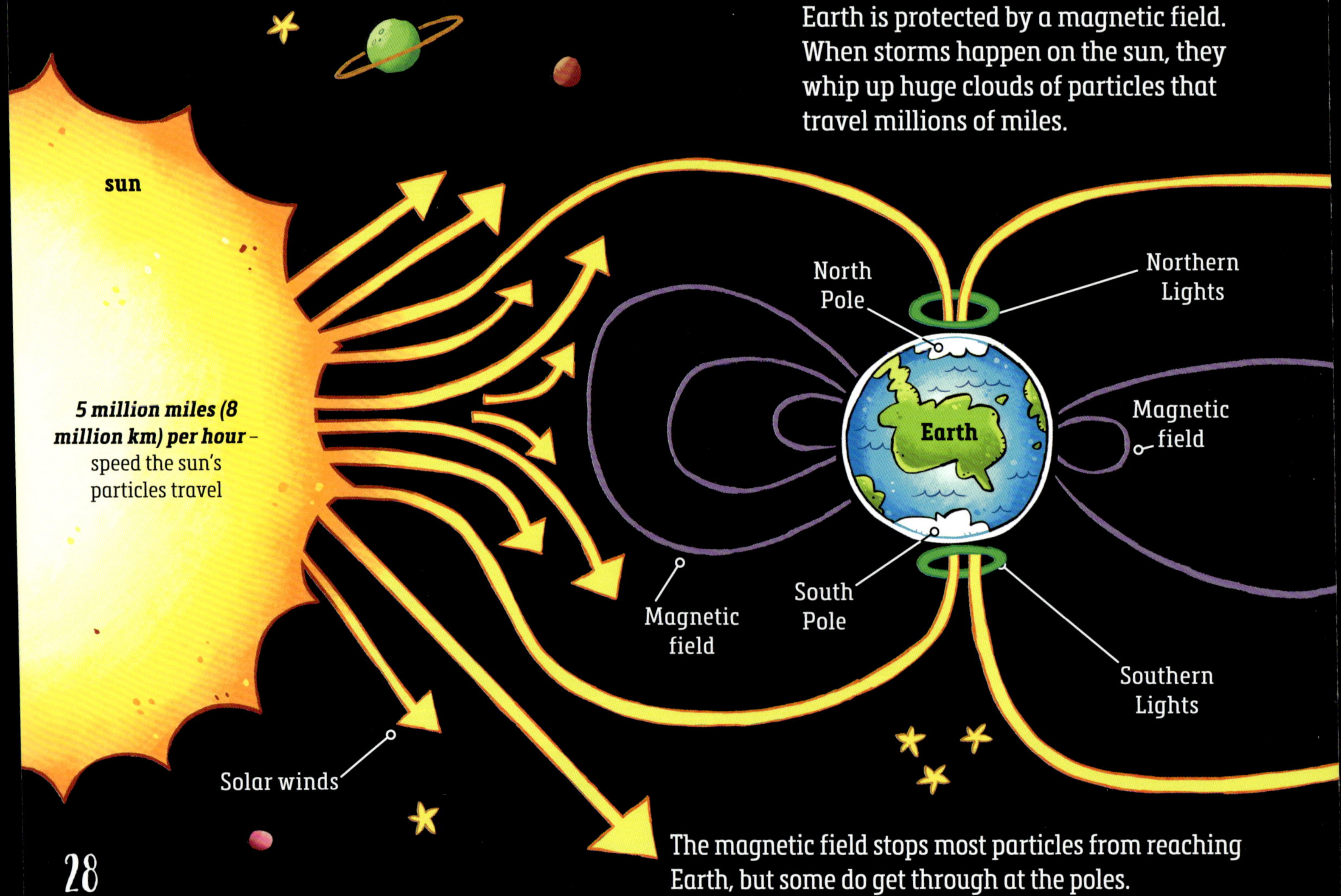

The magnetic field stops most particles from reaching Earth, but some do get through at the poles.

The particles crash into molecules of oxygen and nitrogen in our atmosphere, releasing energy that heats the gases up and makes them glow.

It's like they're dancing **85 miles (135 km)** above us, at a sky-high disco. Different gases make different colors.

We may only see the gases in our atmosphere when the sun's particles make them glow. But they are around us and above us all the time. We could not survive without them.

GLOSSARY

atmosphere – the blanket of gases that surrounds Earth

bacteria – tiny, simple living cells that are too small to see

citrus – a type of tree or shrub that grows citrus fruit, e.g. limes, lemons, oranges, and grapefruit

clean energy – energy that doesn't cause pollution when we use it

climate change – changes in the normal weather on Earth, linked to the warming of the planet due to greenhouse gases

CO_2 – carbon dioxide

digest – the way we process food inside our bodies, breaking it down for energy

emissions – waste substances that are produced and released into the air. They can harm the environment and can harm the environment

EV – electric vehicle

fiber – a substance in certain foods, such as fruit, vegetables, and wheat bread, that travels through the body as waste and helps the contents of the bowels to pass through the body easily

fossil fuel – a fuel such as coal, gas, or oil that formed underground from the remains of plants and animals that died millions of years ago

GHG – greenhouse gas , one of the gases that is building up in Earth's atmosphere and causing climate change

intestines – tubes in the body, between the stomach and the anus, that food passes through

larva – the stage of an insect's life cycle after it hatches from an egg and before it turns into an adult

magnetic field – the area around any kind of magnet that pulls things toward it . Earth's magnetic field stretches out into space.

manufacture – to make or produce something, often in large amounts

microbe – a living thing that is so small it can only be seen through a microscope, such as bacteria or fungi

nitrogen – a gas that you can't see or smell. It makes up 78 percent of Earth's atmosphere

nitrogen oxide – a gas belched out by vehicles that causes air pollution

nitrous oxide – a greenhouse gas which can stay in the atmosphere for 114 years and is 300 times stronger than CO_2

oxygen – a gas that you can't see or taste. Plants and animals all need oxygen to live

paralyze – when something is paralyzed, it can't move or feel

particle – a tiny piece of matter

predator – an animal that hunts and eats other animals

protein – one of the many substances found in food such as meat, cheese, fish, or eggs, that is necessary for the body to grow and be strong

renewable energy – a natural type of energy, such as wind or solar, that does not damage the atmosphere and will never be used up

FURTHER INFORMATION

Books

Comic Strip Science: Chemistry by Paul Mason (Wayland, 2023)

The Farts that Animals Parp by Paul Mason (Gareth Stevens Publishing, 2026)

Websites

Find out more information about the greenhouse effect

climatekids.nasa.gov/greenhouse-effect/

Take a look at the Northern and Southern Lights

seetheaurora.com/webcams

INDEX